GOBSMACKED

GOBSMACKED
Daily Devotions for Advent

Thom Shuman

WILD GOOSE PUBLICATIONS

First published 2011 by
Wild Goose Publications,
Fourth Floor, Savoy House,
140 Sauchiehall Street, Glasgow G2 3DH, UK,
the publishing division of the Iona Community.
Scottish Charity No. SC003794.
Limited Company Reg. No. SC096243.

ISBN 978-1-84952-204-5

Cover design © Wild Goose Publications
Cover photo © David Coleman

The publishers gratefully acknowledge the support of the Drummond Trust,
3 Pitt Terrace, Stirling FK8 2EY in producing this book.

A catalogue record for this book is available from the British Library.

Overseas distribution
Australia: Willow Connection Pty Ltd, Unit 4A, 3-9 Kenneth Road,
Manly Vale, NSW 2093
New Zealand: Pleroma, Higginson Street, Otane 4170, Central Hawkes Bay
Canada: Novalis/Bayard Publishing & Distribution, 10 Lower Spadina Ave.,
Suite 400, Toronto, Ontario M5V 2Z2

Printed by Bell & Bain, Thornliebank, Glasgow

Contents

6

Introduction

For several years now, I have written daily devotions for Advent, sending them out to folks all over the world. Most years, I base them on scripture readings for each day of Advent found in a two-year lectionary in one of the many resource books I use, though occasionally I will pick a reading that is not in that lectionary. This book is a mixture of devotions from several different years.

A word about some of the folks you will meet in these readings. Bonnie is my partner of the past 33 years, my best friend and the light of my life. Teddy is our adult son who, because of his developmental disabilities and mental illness, has spent most of the last 20 years living in a variety of settings for vulnerable persons such as himself. If there is a Christ-figure in my life, it is Teddy – despite the challenges in his life (he is also a survivor of stage four cancer), he continues to take delight in the world around him and to care for those who are even more vulnerable than he is. Heather is Bonnie's sister, who lives near us and who (though she shares her home with 12 cats) loves our dog, Dusty, beyond understanding. And 'Dusty the Church Dog' is a golden retriever we rescued six years ago. He accompanies me to work most days, and takes seriously his job to be the official greeter, the calmer of frayed nerves and worries, and the reader of books to the kids in the preschool. Every day with Dusty, I am reminded that 'dog' is God spelled backwards.

This wee book is for Teddy, Bonnie, Heather, Dusty and all those every-where who journey with me on my pilgrimage.

Thom Shuman

First week of Advent

First Sunday of Advent

To you, O Lord, I lift up my soul.
O my God, in you I trust;
do not let me be put to shame;
do not let my enemies exult over me.
Do not let those who wait for you be put to shame;
let them be ashamed who are wantonly treacherous.

Make me to know your ways, O Lord;
teach me your paths.
Lead me in your truth, and teach me,
for you are the God of my salvation;
for you I wait all day long.

Psalm 25:1–5

The dessert tray

I grew up in a culture which emphasised being a 'meat and potatoes' sort of person. Not just when it came to food for our bodies, but for our souls as well. So, whenever I would go up to the buffet line, I would pile the doctrines on my plate, chewing and chewing until I began to understand ideas like justification, sanctification, Christology … I would go back for seconds of the critiques (historical, textual, contextual) which had been stirred into the servings of scripture readings, hoping they might add a little flavour to my knowledge. But all too often, I left the meal feeling like all I had done was to add a few inches to my theological waistline, and could feel the arteries of my soul harden just a little bit more.

A professor in college once gave me a volume of writings by someone named Julian of Norwich, suggesting, like Professor Lupin to Harry Potter: 'Try it; it's good for you.' Some years later, when I was going through a personal crisis, a friend made a comment about my 'dark night of the soul', and when I looked blank, told me about St John of the Cross. In casual conversations, in sermons, in classes, names like Hildegard and Cuthbert would be dropped; and people would talk about the desert mothers and fathers.

But when I asked for more information, these hermits, these folks who had left the world for the desert or mountain caves, these men and women who had subsisted on very little, seemed to offer a regime that wasn't very appealing, unless you like dry, dusty asceticism.

But these folks kept interrupting my trips to the tables groaning with theology and philosophy. I'd be browsing through a bookstore, and a volume on the abbas and ammas would end up in my hands. I would sit down with a magazine at the library, and find a slim book about Hildegard of Bingen left behind on the chair. A parishioner persistently, and patiently, kept talking to me about Columba and Iona, nudging me until I journeyed there.

So I started reading more of these hermits; I began to immerse myself in the lives and thoughts of Meister Eckhart and Hilda; I would use prayers that came out of the desert, out of the mountainside monasteries, out of the lives of folks who, in 'escaping' from the world, found themselves in God's kingdom. I discovered that these dry, dusty folks were really the rich dessert which God has offered to us over all the centuries.

Now, I spend more time at the dessert bar, putting a slice of Abba Anthony on my plate (sometimes à la Merton). I take a small dish of Hildegard and savour it bite by bite. I take a few pieces of Nouwen home in a doggie bag so I can enjoy them later in the week – for I have discovered the wonders, the joy, the goodness which was so lacking from my meat and potatoes diet.

Some years ago, I found a T-shirt which featured a lot of different flavoured ice cream cones on the front, with the saying on the back 'Life is Short. Eat Dessert First.' Now I just need to find one that says the same thing, but has pictures of the desert mothers and fathers on the front!

Prayer

Baker of our soul's delights, when you come around with the dessert tray, showing us all the marvellous treats your pastry chefs have concocted for us, may we not pretend that we are not hungry enough to take a serving of everything that is prepared for us. Amen

First Monday of Advent

Pray for the peace of Jerusalem:
'May they prosper who love you.
Peace be within your walls,
and security within your towers.'
For the sake of my relatives and friends
I will say, 'Peace be within you.'
For the sake of the house of the Lord our God,
I will seek your good.

Psalm 122:6–9

You are in our midst

This is one of the psalms of Ascents. For untold centuries, those folks journeying to Jerusalem for their annual pilgrimage to the temple would sing, chant or whisper these songs. The evocative nature of these psalms – with their imagery, hopes, prayers, thanksgivings – would speak to the pilgrims of their deepest longings to be in those places where they would find the presence of God resting, waiting for them, like in the Holy of Holies in the temple at Jerusalem.

But when we journey to the hospital, and visit a friend or family member; when we listen to their hopes for recovery, their fears of what the tests might show, their anxiety about undergoing surgery; when we pray for their healing, are we not seeking their good?

When we are behind the counter at the soup kitchen, making sandwiches from the simple gifts provided by others; when we are standing at the stove stirring the soup rich with vegetables and other needed nutrition; when we say a prayer for the food and for those who will be nourished by this feast; when we open the doors and invite them in, and willingly become a part of their lives, listening to their stories, letting them minister to us with their grace and hope, are we not in the Holy of Holies?

When we go down to the local school and work with a 2nd grader who reads at a kindergarten level; when we visit the retirement centre and guide a man's trembling hands as he paints a ceramic angel for his grandchildren's Christmas gift; when we knock on the newly widowed neighbour's door and invite him to Sunday dinner, and listen to his silent grief; when we take our dog for a walk and slow him down from trying to catch a squirrel, so a child can rub his ears until their grins match; when we simply go to all those places where we are surprised to find God already there … aren't we already inside Jerusalem's gate, where God whispers to each and every one of us, 'Peace be within you'?

Prayer

God is in the City

No long, distant pilgrimages are needed, are they, Holiness of our hearts? For you are in our midst, in the people, in the places, in the sounds and silence of our lives. Open our hearts, open our eyes, and quiet us in holy stillness, even as we journey as Advent pilgrims. Amen

First Tuesday of Advent

You remember our labour and toil, brothers and sisters; we worked night and day, so that we might not burden any of you while we proclaimed to you the gospel of God. You are witnesses, and God also, how pure, upright, and blameless our conduct was toward you believers. As you know, we dealt with each one of you like a father with his children, urging and encouraging you and pleading that you lead a life worthy of God, who calls you into his own kingdom and glory.

1 Thessalonians 2:9–12

We know all this

I know what I am called to do as a believer in God. I am invited to live within the boundaries of the kingdom where God's people dwell – where they love and where they hate, where they hurt others as well as where they are damaged by those who love them, where they live in hope and wonder, and where they die, some in pain and some with gentle grace. I know that I am invited to pray for them, for their healing and their peace, with thanksgiving, searching to do good for them always.

I know this, so why don't I *do* it?

You know what journey Jesus is taking you on, when he turns and says, 'Follow me.' You are the ones who hear his challenging stories, his comforting love, his disturbing grace. You are the ones who can't ignore his defiance of the status quo, as he gives his place at the table to the poor, as he invites the illegal immigrant into the circle, as he kisses the child with AIDS. You are the ones he pushes out the door of inner sanctums of piety and dogma. You are the ones he asks to bear witness to the good news that has broken into a damaged world.

You know this, so why are you so reluctant to be called to the witness stand?

We remember that great day when the Spirit came dancing down upon us, filling us with peace, with power, with possibilities spilling out of our hearts. We know that we can become like that nurse who, after his shift is over, goes and sits in the room of the child with cancer, so that her parents can get a good night's sleep. We know that we can be like that mother, bone-weary from standing on her feet for 12 hours, who teaches her 16-year-old how to slow dance, so he won't be embarrassed at the winter prom. We know that the life we lead can provide a path for others who seem to have lost their way.

We know all this, yet we all too often act as if we have become amnesiacs, don't we?

Prayer

We no longer have any excuses to give, Loving God, in this time of great worry and calamity. We must show that we *do* know how to live as your people. Help us not to forget all that you have taught us. Amen

First Wednesday of Advent

As for us, brothers and sisters, when, for a short time, we were made orphans by being separated from you – in person, not in heart – we longed with great eagerness to see you face to face. For we wanted to come to you – certainly I, Paul, wanted to again and again – but Satan blocked our way. For what is our hope or joy or crown of boasting before our Lord Jesus at his coming? Is it not you? Yes, you are our glory and joy!

1 Thessalonians 2:17–20

Face to face

I'd love to see Dan this Christmas, my best friend in (and after) college. It has to be 15 years or more since we've seen each other, and that was when he, Jodi, and the family had a layover at the airport here in Cincinnati. Whenever we would see each other after an absence, it seemed as if, once we started talking, all that missing time of being apart just melted away, and we were back in the dorm, continuing a conversation we began nearly 50 years ago when we entered college together. But they are out on the West Coast, and that's a long, long way – especially for someone who would rather have root canal than fly. But, I'll bet if I got to look into his face, he'd look the same!

And it would be a special Christmas indeed, if I could sit down around the dinner table with the Millers. To be with Robert and Nancy, with John, Margaret, Helen and Francis, with their spouses and kids – what a joy that would be. Looking into faces lined with wonder and worry, comparing the grey and white hairs caused by kids and the kindness of God, to simply enjoy the comfortable silence that we can share with one another – that would be one of the best gifts I could have this year. But they (like so many families) are scattered, and with the economy the way it is, it probably won't happen.

I'd like to look into my mother's face this year, to see it, as I always do, through the eyes of a child who thinks his mother is the wisest, the most beautiful, the most gentle person in the world (and she is, believe me). I'd like to sit down with my siblings and reconnect, to find out what has *really* been going on in their lives over the last few years, to behold them face to face. I'd like to see my nieces and nephews, especially Scot, who just got back, safely, thank God, from serving overseas. But we are scattered, we are busy, two of us have to 'work' on Christmas Eve.

But the boss who, when I said I was resigning from university work in order to go to seminary, told me: 'Well, those who can, do; those who can't do, teach; those who can't teach, go into ministry'? Not sure if I would want to sit down and exchange Christmas cards with him.

And the folks at one church who made life such a hell for me and my family over the last 18 months, who treated me with such disrespect, and spoke words no person, much less a Christian, should speak? I am not sure if I could sit down around any table with them this Christmas.

In my mind's eye, there is a long line of people whom I would just rather not see face to face at this time of year. It would be too painful, too hard, too depressing for such a season …

Yet, this is the season when we celebrate that amazing grace of God, who was willing to come to be one of us. Who was willing to live with, to encounter, to eat with those who would ridicule and reject him, who would hurt him, who would even kill him. And God was willing to look at them face to face and simply say: *'I forgive you; I love you; I came for you.'*

Prayer

How easy it is to long to look into the faces of those we love or we know love us. Strengthen us to look into the faces we would rather avoid, and to be able to see your Child in them, even as we seek to show that he lives in us. Amen

First Thursday of Advent

In days to come
the mountain of the Lord's house
shall be established as the highest of the mountains,
and shall be raised above the hills;
all the nations shall stream to it.
Many peoples shall come and say,
'Come, let us go up to the mountain of the Lord,
to the house of the God of Jacob;
that he may teach us his ways
and that we may walk in his paths.'
For out of Zion shall go forth instruction,
and the word of the Lord from Jerusalem.
He shall judge between the nations,
and shall arbitrate for many peoples;
they shall beat their swords into ploughshares,
and their spears into pruning hooks;
nation shall not lift up sword against nation,
neither shall they learn war any more.

O house of Jacob,
come, let us walk
in the light of the Lord!

Isaiah 2:2–5

The voice of Odetta

I would lie in the dark of my dorm room in college and listen to her low voice singing:

> 'No more auction block for me,
> no more, no more …
> No more auction block for me,
> many thousand gone.'

After listening to the likes of Ramblin' Jack Elliot, Pete Seeger, Woody Guthrie, I discovered the voice of Odetta, a voice of wisdom, a voice of spirituality, a voice for conscience, a voice for freedom.

She marched with Martin Luther King, Jr, and stood on the steps of the Lincoln Memorial in August 1963 singing 'O Freedom' – and all one could say was 'Oh yes!' She experienced the success and adulation which her voice could bring her, and she experienced those deep, deep wounds that others inflicted on her because of the colour of her skin. Her voice was sometimes so low you might make the mistake of thinking you were listening to a man singing. But the unique timbre of her voice was her passion for justice, for equality, for change.

Like Isaiah, she saw that vision God has of a time, and a place, and a people who could be at peace, who would live for justice, who would have open doors and open tables where every single one of God's children was welcome. She was passionately committed to the notion that people could walk in God's light, because she had been relegated to the shadows by the culture in which she lived as a young person in Alabama. She believed that it wasn't just words in a dusty book sitting on the pulpit in an empty church, but that it was possible for guns to be turned into guitars, for tanks to be dismantled and converted into school buses, for war colleges to become retirement homes for pacifists.

Dr King called her 'the Queen of American folk music'. She was an influence on other singers – from Bob Dylan to Janis Joplin, from Joan Baez to John Hiatt. When Rosa Parks was asked what songs meant the most to her, she simply replied, 'All the songs Odetta sings.' And she was scheduled to sing at the inauguration of Barack Obama, before her untimely death.

So, who will sing the songs God taught to Isaiah and Odetta now?

Prayer

The sheet music may be yellowed with age and curling at the corners; the instruments may be slightly out of tune; the harmonies may sound discordant; the words may need to be updated just a bit – but songs of justice are needed in every age, carols about compassion can be easily learned by the smallest child, hymns of hope are there in the memories of our grandparents, just longing to burst forth. Amen

First Friday of Advent

Hear my prayer, O Lord;
let my cry come to you.
Do not hide your face from me
in the day of my distress.

Psalm 102:1–2

Finally, brothers and sisters, we ask and urge you in the Lord Jesus that, as you learned from us how you ought to live and to please God (as, in fact, you are doing), you should do so more and more …

For God did not call us to impurity but in holiness. Therefore whoever rejects this rejects not human authority but God, who also gives his Holy Spirit to you. Now concerning love of the brothers and sisters, you do not need to have anyone write to you, for you yourselves have been taught by God to love one another; and indeed you do love all the brothers and sisters throughout Macedonia. But we urge you, beloved, to do so more and more, to aspire to live quietly, to mind your own affairs, and to work with your hands, as we directed you, so that you may behave properly toward outsiders and be dependent on no one.

1 Thessalonians 4:1–2, 7–12

The people of Advent

God calls us to holiness, Paul tells us, and in this holy season, we prepare to live such lives. Lives that are lived quietly, yet do more and more for those God invites us to serve. Lives that focus on looking after our own affairs, yet being willing to use our hands, our hearts, our souls on behalf of others. A holiness that invites us to draw closer to God, in love and hope, and teaches us how to treat those the world rejects and considers to be outsiders.

Some of this we already know. After all as people of faith, however feeble or full, we have learned the Ten Commandments, we are taught the Golden Rule. We have been taught that we should 'do justice, love kindness, and walk humbly with God'. We have heard the sermons and Sunday school discussions about 'letting justice roll forth like a raging river'. With the little children, we can sing of how Jesus loves us, and how Jesus loves all the children of God. We know so much and so live out lives of great know-i-ness.

But do we know how to please God? Have we discovered those insights, those intuitive flashes, those inner disciplines that allow us to know, yes, but, more importantly, *to be* (as God intends) the sort of people who hear the owl hooting in the wilderness; who see the teenager sitting at the mall like a lonely bird, while the rest of the flock is twittering away; who notice the heart-stricken face of the neighbour reading a letter from their dearest friend; who are willing to share a sandwich with one whose life has turned to ashes?

For these are the people we live with, we drive next to on the way to work, we sit with in a classroom, we brush past in the card store, we jostle elbows with as we juggle our packages at the post office. These are the people who look for a friend in every person, but see only blank faces. These are the people who hunger for affirmation, but hear only grumblings and mutterings under the breath. These are the people whose poverty of spirit could be filled by the simple act of a kind smile.

These are the people of Advent. The ones God has come for in Christ, and the ones God would have us come to know, as intimately, as lovingly, as gently as we want God to know us.

Prayer

Help us to please you, Wise God, not by reciting all the verses we have memorised, all the theology we have learned, all the knowledge we have attained. But by living lives of kindness, of justice, of love – for these are the signs of true holiness, the signs we see in the One who came for us that first Advent so long ago.

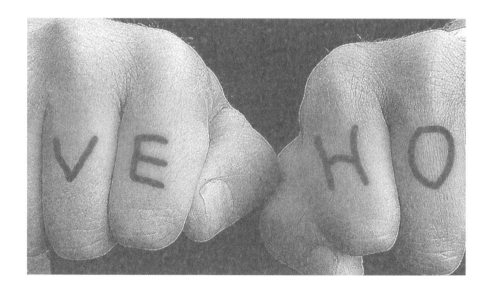

First Saturday of Advent

When some were speaking about the temple, how it was adorned with beautiful stones and gifts dedicated to God, he said, 'As for these things that you see, the days will come when not one stone will be left upon another; all will be thrown down.'

They asked him, 'Teacher, when will this be, and what will be the sign that this is about to take place?' And he said, 'Beware that you are not led astray; for many will come in my name and say, "I am he!" and, "The time is near!" Do not go after them.

'When you hear of wars and insurrections, do not be terrified; for these things must take place first, but the end will not follow immediately.' Then he said to them, 'Nation will rise against nation, and kingdom against kingdom; there will be great earthquakes, and in various places famines and plagues; and there will be dreadful portents and great signs from heaven.

'But before all this occurs, they will arrest you and persecute you; they will hand you over to synagogues and prisons, and you will be brought before kings and governors because of my name. This will give you an opportunity to testify. So make up your minds not to prepare your defence in advance; for I will give you words and a wisdom that none of your opponents will be able to withstand or contradict. You will be betrayed even by parents and brothers, by relatives and friends; and they will put some of you to death. You will be hated by all because of my name. But not a hair of your head will perish. By your endurance you will gain your souls.'

Luke 21:5–19

Fear and endurance

At the age of 14, I went through confirmation class in order to become a member of the church. I didn't do it because I wanted to serve on a board, or get to vote at meetings, or even be on the mailing list for the stewardship campaign. I did it because I was afraid. For I lived in a time and culture which made it pretty clear that if I did not profess Jesus Christ as my Lord and Saviour, if I didn't sign on the dotted line as a member of the church, if I didn't stand up and let myself be counted, well, then there was only one destination for me when I died.

Fear can be a powerful motivator. Politicians know it, and use it at the first hint of any trouble. Teachers know it, and use it to get the kids to stay in line. Parents know it, and can cause it by the look in the eye, or the lifting of a hand. And, sadly, religious folks know this truth as well. I think that is why there is a segment of Christianity which finds passages like this one in Luke to be perhaps the most important words Jesus spoke. After all, if we can get folks to take seriously a fearful notion of the End Times, to worry about being left behind, to know without a single doubt that they run a great risk of being stuck on earth to live through the great tribulation, then the pews can be filled, as well as the coffers.

But while fear can make us alert when we are walking through a graveyard at midnight; while fear can give us the adrenalin to get through the long days of worrying about a child facing a life-threatening illness; while fear can make us drop a bad habit, and lead a healthier life, fear can only be a motivator, can only drive us, for just a little while. Truth be told, fear has a very short shelf life.

But endurance?

It's that dogged determination to get out of bed on a snowy, frigid Saturday and show up for that tutoring session with a bunch of neighbour kids. It's that stubborn willingness to keep talking to your kids about faith: that there is something more to life than just Facebook and iPods, that there is Someone who is not going to disappoint them or reject them or make them feel like complete idiots; and when they ask you for tangible, rational, touchable proof, to say with wonder, and simplicity, 'It's a mystery.'

It's that belief that spending time in prayer will become more than practice, it will become a way of listening to God and noticing God's presence in others. It's that faithful act of sitting through soul-numbing sermons, because God has promised to speak through the Word. It's that foolish and antiquated notion, in today's world, of letting one's decisions be guided by a relationship with Someone who will never show up on the television talk show circuit. It's that understanding that while scripture may not be literal, inerrant words from God, it can be trusted for faith and practice.

Jesus doesn't tell us at the end of these apocalyptic visions that our fear will help us to gain our souls, but our endurance. That endurance that is modelled for us by the One who kept journeying towards Jerusalem, to the Cross. That endurance which is shared with us by those who do not let cancer, job loss, grief break them. That endurance which, Paul reminds us, shapes our character, and turns us into people of hope, people of Advent.

Prayer

Whether it is persecution or panic attacks, you give us those gifts which help us to endure. Whether facing fear or foolishness, you surround us with folks who can help us to endure. Continue to put up with us, Approaching God, as we struggle to be your people. Amen

Second week of Advent

Second Sunday of Advent

The beginning of the good news of Jesus Christ, the Son of God.

As it is written in the prophet Isaiah,
'See, I am sending my messenger ahead of you,
who will prepare your way;
the voice of one crying out in the wilderness:
"Prepare the way of the Lord,
make his paths straight,"'

John the baptiser appeared in the wilderness, proclaiming a baptism of repentance for the forgiveness of sins. And people from the whole Judean countryside and all the people of Jerusalem were going out to him, and were baptised by him in the river Jordan, confessing their sins. Now John was clothed with camel's hair, with a leather belt around his waist, and he ate locusts and wild honey. He proclaimed, 'The one who is more powerful than I is coming after me; I am not worthy to stoop down and untie the thong of his sandals. I have baptised you with water; but he will baptise you with the Holy Spirit.'

Mark 1:1–8

Dusty's world

While our golden retriever, Dusty, is known throughout blogdom as 'the Church Dog', at home he is affectionately called COTU –

Centre Of The Universe!

And he certainly acts like it at times. The only reason we get out of bed in the morning is so that he can get his food, and be let outside so he can sit on the front lawn and survey his domain. We come home, simply so that we can take him for a walk, throw a ball for him and, of course, feed him. And anyone who comes to the door, be it friend or neighbour, be it a young person selling candy for her school or the plumber, they have come to play with him, to admire him, to let him know how beautiful and wonderful he is.

Oh yes, in Dusty's world, it is all about him!

I am beginning to wonder if that attitude – if that sense of being COTU – hasn't crept into the church.

Someone says that our church is dwindling and if it closes, there will be no one else to do what we have been doing for the last 50, 150, 1500 years. Really?

A study proclaims that by the year (take your pick), the mainline denominations will have disappeared, and we talk as if at that point Christianity will disappear from the face of the earth.

A Moderator, a theologian, an author, an 'expert' speaks at a seminar, and offers the 9-step programme to becoming the most successful, the most popular (and populous), the most well-known congregation in the country, and we drop all the faithful missions and ministries we have been working at to serve God's people, in order to be first in line to buy the new programme.

Well, maybe it's not all about us. Maybe it's not all about a particular church staying open. Maybe it's not all about a denomination which has become outdated and outmoded.

Maybe, as Mark says, it's about the Gospel. The Gospel of Jesus Christ. It's not about my sermons, or her music, or our successes.

Maybe, as Mark says, we are not called to be entrepreneurs, or emerging prophets, or one of the Top 10 preachers listed in *Time Magazine*. No, it's about being forerunners, messengers, friends of the bridegroom, pointing past ourselves and all our pretensions, all our insecurities – to Jesus. Maybe, as Mark says, we are living in the beginning of the Gospel of Jesus Christ, the Son of God.

Prayer

Stick a pin in our puffed-up pride, bring us down just a few pegs, stuff our stockings with little nuggets of humility rather than award us with all the blue ribbons we think we have earned; and in doing so, remind us of the good, good news we are blessed to share with everyone we know, and don't. Amen

Second Monday of Advent

Praise the Lord!
How good it is to sing praises to our God;
for he is gracious, and a song of praise is fitting.
The Lord builds up Jerusalem;
he gathers the outcasts of Israel.
He heals the brokenhearted,
and binds up their wounds.
He determines the number of the stars;
he gives to all of them their names.
Great is our Lord, and abundant in power;
his understanding is beyond measure.
The Lord lifts up the downtrodden;
he casts the wicked to the ground.

Sing to the Lord with thanksgiving;
make melody to our God on the lyre.

Psalm 147:1–7

The lost art

It's undeniable that music is a major force during this season of holiness. Whether it is the annual 'battle' over when a church can begin to sing the beloved carols, or churches bringing in brass or string groups for worship, or choirs of little children being taught how not to fidget and the appropriate use of hands while singing at the family service, music is foundational for the observance of the celebration of the Christ Child.

Yet, do you notice that for most of us, the music comes from someone else other than ourselves?

It is piped into the stores, the elevators, the Underground. It is a professional group, or the chancel choir, or the Little Cherubs, who are doing the singing. It is special concerts down at the square, or in the music hall, or on television, or on our iPods. But it is not usually us, who are going around singing.

We've lost the art of singing, I'm afraid. There was a time in our past when people were singing all the time. Fathers sang lullabies to their babies, mothers sang 'My Lord, What a Morning' while getting ready for the day. Families sang around the dinner table, or in the family room in the evening. People sang while building bridges, working at a lathe, sweeping the front porch, weeding the garden, doing laundry, mowing the lawn. Whether it was hymns or a show tune, a psalm or a pop standard, people went around singing. But not any more.

Nearly a century ago, John Philip Sousa remarked, 'What will happen to the American voice now that they've invented the phonograph?' And I can only imagine his reaction to iPods that can hold hundreds of songs – everyone walking around with their own headphones, listening to their own music, not noticing all those others flowing down that same street, with their ears filled with *their own* private stock of tunes.

As Pete Seeger was fond of saying: music is full of great power. Yes, it can help us forget our troubles. Yes, like the psalms, those marvellous songs filled with the full range of human experience and emotion, music can help us to understand our troubles.

But, Seeger goes on to say, music can help us to *do something* about our troubles. Music can bring us together with folks who are just as broken as we are, and we can draw comfort and strength as we sing 'sometimes I feel like a motherless child'. Music can put us in touch with those who have experienced the same suffering as we have, yet together we can dance to a lively klezmer tune. Music can unite us with those who long for justice and an end to every form of human oppression, and we can lift our voices in 'We Shall Overcome' as we march, and work and vote.

Maybe this year, we should start singing again. Start out slowly, in the shower or in the car. Hum a tune on the bus or the subway car (and notice if anyone starts humming along with you!). Sing along with Perry, or Toby, or Beyoncé, or your favourite group. Turn off the TV, and gather around the piano instead.

But sing, sing, sing … praising God for the wonderful gift of music, echoing the songs sung on that first morning of the new creation so long ago.

Prayer

Whether with a piano or an old kazoo, whether classical or country, whether solo or with a friend, we would sing to you, Joyous Heart, as we wait to celebrate your coming to us. Amen

Second Tuesday of Advent

When the day of Pentecost had come, they were all together in one place. And suddenly from heaven there came a sound like the rush of a violent wind, and it filled the entire house where they were sitting. Divided tongues, as of fire, appeared among them, and a tongue rested on each of them. All of them were filled with the Holy Spirit and began to speak in other languages, as the Spirit gave them ability.

Acts 2:1–4

But we appeal to you, brothers and sisters, to respect those who labour among you, and have charge of you in the Lord and admonish you; esteem them very highly in love because of their work. Be at peace among yourselves. And we urge you, beloved, to admonish the idlers, encourage the fainthearted, help the weak, be patient with all of them. See that none of you repays evil for evil, but always seek to do good to one another and to all. Rejoice always, pray without ceasing, give thanks in all circumstances; for this is the will of God in Christ Jesus for you. Do not quench the Spirit. Do not despise the words of prophets

1 Thessalonians 5:12–20

New people, new voices, new hearts

So often, it seems that the church has installed sprinklers throughout the building, not for safety reasons, but so that there is no danger of what happened on that first day of Pentecost taking place – in our churches, in our people, in our lives. We have to make sure there is no explosion of excitement, no flare-up of faith, no gust of grace blowing through our halls. We are committed to playing it safe, to remaining calm, to keeping a tight rein on our little piece of the kingdom.

A young adult takes on the task of working with the youth in a church. Intelligent, enthusiastic, faithful, committed to creating a space where kids can safely explore the Bible, talk about the world in which they live, struggle with the choices they face, he begins to engage with the kids in a way which is attractive and meaningful to them. Yet, because he is not offering the same sort of structure and programming that was done years ago, he is criticised. *Splash*!

A musician attends a conference where she is challenged by the variety of musical programmes and offerings. Exposed to new ways of praising God – with different tunes, instruments, languages, voices – she catches a vision of what the psalmists mean when they talk about 'new songs for God'. Determined to bring these gifts to her choir and congregation, she is confronted with comments about the tunes not being singable, about the words not being in English, about the songs not being in the hymnal. *Slosh*!

Several members are approached to serve on a committee. Not sure why the church would want them, but assured that they are precisely what the group needs, they reluctantly agree. After several meetings of giving their input, but not seeing it appear in the minutes; of offering suggestions for new ways of doing things, but being told that the way it was done the last few years still works; of providing creative ideas on some different ministries and missions, but never hearing them put to the governing board, they come to realise they were asked solely so the committee would have a full complement of people. *Douse*.

Maybe that is why, in writing to one of the first congregations of the early church, the apostle Paul urged them to rejoice, to pray, to give thanks and, in a warning to every generation, 'do not quench the Spirit'.

Prayer

When we are tempted to throw water on all the new ideas your Spirit offers to us through new people, new voices, new hearts, Surprising God, help us to sit down, take a cool drink, and listen, just listen – to them, and to you. Amen

Second Wednesday of Advent

In the year that King Uzziah died, I saw the Lord sitting on a throne, high and lofty; and the hem of his robe filled the temple. Seraphs were in attendance above him; each had six wings: with two they covered their faces, and with two they covered their feet, and with two they flew. And one called to another and said:

'Holy, holy, holy is the Lord of hosts;
the whole earth is full of his glory.'

The pivots on the thresholds shook at the voices of those who called, and the house filled with smoke. And I said: 'Woe is me! I am lost, for I am a man of unclean lips, and I live among a people of unclean lips; yet my eyes have seen the King, the Lord of hosts!'

Then one of the seraphs flew to me, holding a live coal that had been taken from the altar with a pair of tongs. The seraph touched my mouth with it and said: 'Now that this has touched your lips, your guilt has departed and your sin is blotted out.' Then I heard the voice of the Lord saying, 'Whom shall I send, and who will go for us?' And I said, 'Here am I; send me!'

Isaiah 6:1–8

The One who calls us

By all the standards of his day, he was on his way to success. Bright, articulate, popular with his friends and colleagues, he probably would have been a great professor, a scholar, an author, a mentor. But on December 10, 1941, Thomas Merton entered the monastic life at the Abbey of Gethsemani. Though he had been expressing an interest in developing his faith in his adult years, and was especially drawn to those saints with deep contemplative roots, his friends were still surprised by his decision to enter a life of poverty and make a commitment to one particular community for the rest of his life. Yet for Merton, it felt like he had finally arrived home. And 27 years later, when he died on December 10, 1968, he had indeed become a great teacher, a scholar, an author, a mentor – a spiritual guide who continues to speak to millions of people throughout the world today.

No one can really put into words why or how they are called to lives of faith. For some, it is a journey home; for others, it is the feeling of being chased by God. For some, it is a dramatic epiphany such as Isaiah speaks about; for others, it is a dawning awareness of how God wishes them to use their gifts. For some, it is a call to leave everything behind and enter a world of silence and prayer; for others it is a job filled with meetings and paperwork. For some, it is lived out as a pastor or priest; for others, it is a life of teaching, of mothering, of laying bricks, of nursing care, of sitting at a keyboard … But, like Merton, each of us is called to follow, to live out our faith, to finally find that place God has called us to to be a servant.

A few years ago, a friend asked me to write a prayer for her ordination to ministry. While I wrote it for a specific person, called to a particular place, perhaps it speaks to all of us who seek to listen and to keep on listening to the One who calls us.

who –
me?

called
to look foolish
so others might
discover you;

called
to become weak
so your hurting children
might be touched
by your healing heart;
so those who weep
by cold graves
might feel your
warmth comforting them;

called
to speak
(not in six-syllable lectures)
but to whisper
your simple words
grace   hope
peace   joy
love   life
those teeny-tiny seeds
of your heart
nourished with cold cups

of living water,
growing into gracefulness,
embracing and welcoming
all;

who –
me?

here i am, Lord:

sent here.

Second Thursday of Advent

For God alone my soul waits in silence;
from him comes my salvation.
He alone is my rock and my salvation,
my fortress; I shall never be shaken …

For God alone my soul waits in silence,
for my hope is from him.
He alone is my rock and my salvation,
my fortress; I shall not be shaken.
On God rests my deliverance and my honour;
my mighty rock, my refuge is in God.

Psalm 62:1–2, 5–7

Learning to play the silence

Mr Pete, the Drum Man, comes every year for Vacation Bible School – and the kids are always thrilled! They get to play on different sizes of drums, and learn something about rhythm. Perhaps not so surprising: the girls seem interested in the different tones the drums make; the boys just want to be the loudest!

This is Mr Pete's ministry. As he exposes kids to the sound of the drums, their texture, their tones, he is introducing them to the Gospel. He talks about how the kids (and the lucky adults who are with them) become a part of a family: the Drum Circle. Every drum has a different voice and every voice is important to the circle. And just as every voice is important to the circle, every voice is important to a community of faith, and needs to be included, heard and valued. Every drum has a part to play, and when one drum makes a mistake, the next drum helps to bring it back into life's rhythm.

But Pete also teaches them about silence. In the teaching of a particular rhythm, he puts in a measure of silence. *Boom, boom-boom, boom, boom-boom, silence, boom.* And he has us hold our hands up in the air to play the silence. And Pete believes, as I think Jesus does, that silence is the hardest note to play – on any instrument: drums, piano, voice, life. But the silence is as important as all the sounds we make, and Pete wants the kids to listen to the sound that the silence can create.

Some people think that Jesus went away from the crowds and the disciples to recharge his batteries, to get some rest, to take a retreat, to be closer to God, to pray. All possibilities, which few of us do ourselves. Me, I think he went away to listen to the silence he was trying to play in his heart.

We know how to be loud, we know how to soften our voices. We know how to argue, and we know how to whisper. We know how to talk and talk and talk. We know how to use words to intimidate, to manipulate, to criticise; we know how to play our voices so people will feel sorry for us, or love us, or want to rescue us.

But when do we learn how to play the silence?

Instead of a spoken prayer, just spend some time in silence …

Second Friday of Advent

When the hour came, he took his place at the table, and the apostles with him. He said to them, 'I have eagerly desired to eat this Passover with you before I suffer; for I tell you, I will not eat it until it is fulfilled in the kingdom of God.' Then he took a cup, and after giving thanks he said, 'Take this and divide it among yourselves; for I tell you that from now on I will not drink of the fruit of the vine until the kingdom of God comes.' Then he took a loaf of bread, and when he had given thanks, he broke it and gave it to them, saying, 'This is my body, which is given for you. Do this in remembrance of me.' And he did the same with the cup after supper, saying, 'This cup that is poured out for you is the new covenant in my blood. But see, the one who betrays me is with me, and his hand is on the table. For the Son of Man is going as it has been determined, but woe to that one by whom he is betrayed!' Then they began to ask one another which one of them it could be who would do this.

A dispute also arose among them as to which one of them was to be regarded as the greatest. But he said to them, 'The kings of the Gentiles lord it over them; and those in authority over them are called benefactors. But not so with you; rather the greatest among you must become like the youngest, and the leader like one who serves. For who is greater, the one who is at the table or the one who serves? Is it not the one at the table? But I am among you as one who serves.'

Luke 22:14–27

In all the nows to come

We should reach critical mass sometime next week. With Christmas Day getting closer and closer, with more and more activities at school, with meetings almost every night, the annual meltdown should take place soon (mid-week is my best guess). There is just too much to do. It's the same thing at the church. More services to prepare, several newsletter articles to be submitted, end of the year 'business'. And people can share their gifts in an amazing variety of ways. In addition to the choir, worship, governing board, pot luck dinner, there is the host of voices singing of their needs – trees on which to hang mittens; hats and scarves for those who have none; food collections; a box for toys, books, school supplies; opportunities to give to any number of charities, sacred and secular. There is just too much to do.

Yet, in the background, where they always have been and always will be, are the hungry and homeless, the wandering and wondering, the families who must choose between food or medicine, the lost, the last, the least, the little who are such an intimate part of Jesus's family. The ones whose needs continue every day, every week, every month, not through any fault of theirs, it is just the way of the world.

But this is the way of the world Jesus came to change, this is the world Jesus came to challenge. Recognising that the hunger will grow and the available food will diminish, knowing that the winter winds will continue to slice through lives and the coatbox will be empty, aware of the kids who go to bed each night scared and lonely – Jesus tells us he is among us as one who serves.

Not just during a month, but through a lifetime; not just on his birthday, but through his death; not just in the season of joy and giving, but in the years of emptiness and despair. He is among us as one who serves, and he simply hopes that we will join him, not just now, but in all the *nows* to come.

Prayer

You came to serve, Blessing of Bethlehem, in all places, to all your children, through all your followers. Help us to continue to serve at your side. Amen

Second Saturday of Advent

And Mary said,
'My soul magnifies the Lord,
and my spirit rejoices in God my Saviour,
for he has looked with favour on the lowliness of his servant.
Surely, from now on all generations will call me blessed;
for the Mighty One has done great things for me,
and holy is his name.
His mercy is for those who fear him
from generation to generation.
He has shown strength with his arm;
he has scattered the proud in the thoughts of their hearts.
He has brought down the powerful from their thrones,
and lifted up the lowly;
he has filled the hungry with good things,
and sent the rich away empty.
He has helped his servant Israel,
in remembrance of his mercy,
according to the promise he made to our ancestors,
to Abraham and to his descendants forever.'

Luke 1:46–55

Praises piggyback

While Lizzie started making dinner, Mary slipped out the back door and wandered down to the frozen pond. Sitting down on the rough-hewn bench that Zeke had made a few summers before, she stared across the ice towards the hillside where the shepherds were huddled for warmth around a fire, while the sheep shuffled, trying to get comfortable in the chill air.

'What a strange few weeks,' she muttered to herself. She thought back to her conversation with the stranger at the bus stop while she waited to go home after doing her homework at the library. She kept trying to inch away from him, until there was no more inching she could do, stunned at his repeated insistence that she was going to have a child (*hey*, she had thought to herself, *I'm a good girl!*) and the child would be a gift from God. Actually, he had said the baby would be God. What can one say to that?! 'Sure, whatever you say, mister' was all she could come up with.

Snapping out of her reverie, she began to rummage around in her backpack, pulling out her skates. As she wiped the blades clean, she relived the chat she had just had with her auntie. How in the world did Lizzie figure out she was pregnant – she herself had just found out the other day! And, wonder of wonders, Lizzie was going to have a kid, too – at her age! She must be near 40. And she thinks I am blessed!

She slipped off her right shoe, put on the skate, and began to tighten the laces. She giggled to herself, as she remembered how she and Sarah had talked late one night, after Shabbos dinner. Like all kids, they wondered what the Anointed One would be like when he came. 'When Messiah comes,' Sarah had whispered, 'I hope he comes as a baker, with wonderful goodies and lots of hot bread for everyone. I am so tired of being hungry all the time.'

Finished tying that skate, she quickly put on her left one, as she remembered what her boyfriend, Joseph, had said to her, while they walked home from the synagogue one day. 'The rabbi uses such big words, I can't always understand him. I'm a simple man,' he said, gazing into her eyes he could not pull himself away from. 'I want someone who can tell me in plain terms about Adonai. Who can put his thoughts into words a carpenter like me can hear, so that I can then walk away saying, "*Now* I see".'

Stretching her neck and shoulder muscles, loosening up her arms and legs, she stared off into the blue-black sky, freckled with stars which glimmered in the crisp night. 'I just want mercy – sweet, tender mercy when Messiah comes. Compassion for all the children whose parents have no time for them; help for those who long to shelter and feed their families, but who have no money; hope for those who clasp those promises made so long ago to Sarah and Abraham, and wait so patiently for them to come true.'

Stepping out onto the ice, she slowly began to do her warm-ups, circles and figure eights, beginning to hum a little tune which she did not recognise, but had just popped into her head. As she picked up speed on the ice, she started to murmur words which tumbled out of her heart, in rhythm to the tune:

> *praises piggyback*
> > *until my soul topples over;*
> *i toast my God,*
> > *taking great gulps of joy.*
> > *Listening with compassion,*
> > *she pours a cup of coffee*
> > > *for the footsore waitress,*
> > > > *softly whistling 'O Holy Night'.*
> *Like a grandmother to a daughter,*
> > *like a mother to a son,*

she teaches the cross-stitch pattern
of mercy
to all who want to learn.
After lifting weights
down at Grace's Gym,
God grabs a push-broom
to whisk out the garbage
of our minds;
tapping the lobbyists
on the shoulder,
and escorting them
to the children's table,
the immigrants are given
the seats at the head table;
God crams a suite of hope
into our unfurnished souls,
and takes the shoes
off the well-heeled
so the outcasts can walk
the streets of the kingdom.
Reminiscing at the dinner table
about our grandparents,
God memorises our faces
so we can fill her dreams at night.

Third week of Advent

Third Sunday of Advent

There was a man sent from God, whose name was John. He came as a witness to testify to the light, so that all might believe through him. He himself was not the light, but he came to testify to the light …

This is the testimony given by John when the Jews sent priests and Levites from Jerusalem to ask him, 'Who are you?' He confessed and did not deny it, but confessed, 'I am not the Messiah.' And they asked him, 'What then? Are you Elijah?' He said, 'I am not.' 'Are you the prophet?' He answered, 'No.' Then they said to him, 'Who are you? Let us have an answer for those who sent us. What do you say about yourself?' He said,

'I am the voice of one crying out in the wilderness,
"Make straight the way of the Lord,"'
as the prophet Isaiah said.

Now they had been sent from the Pharisees. They asked him, 'Why then are you baptising if you are neither the Messiah, nor Elijah, nor the prophet? John answered them, 'I baptise with water. Among you stands one whom you do not know, the one who is coming after me; I am not worthy to untie the thong of his sandal.' This took place in Bethany across the Jordan where John was baptising …

Now a discussion about purification arose between John's disciples and a Jew. They came to John and said to him, 'Rabbi, the one who was with you across the Jordan, to whom you testified, here he is baptising, and all are going to him.' John answered, 'No one can receive anything except what has been given from heaven. You yourselves are my witnesses that I said, "I am not the Messiah, but I have been sent ahead of him." He who has the bride is the bridegroom. The friend of the bridegroom, who stands and hears him, rejoices greatly at the bridegroom's voice. For this reason my joy has been fulfilled. He must increase, but I must decrease.'

John 1:6–8, 19–28; 3:25–30

Friend of the bridegroom

'This room will come to order,' the Chair intones. 'This hearing is for the purpose of obtaining the facts concerning this person who has appeared in our midst, who seems to be causing a great deal of controversy among our people. The first witness has been sworn in. Would you please identify yourself for this committee?'

'I am called John the Baptist.'

Shuffling some papers until he finds the right document, the Chair asks, 'Mr Baptist, are you the light that has come into the world?'

'No, Senator, I am not. And please, call me John.'

'If you are not the light, then who are you?'

'I am simply the one who draws people from the shadows of this world, and of their lives, so they can find the Light.'

'Well then, are you this word we have heard about, that is supposed to have been from the beginning of all time?'

'No, I am not the Word. But for all those folks who have been deafened by all the noise of our culture, I hope my words will lead them to the One who can silence their fears, who can speak to their concerns, who can answer their questions, who can whisper songs of joy and peace into their ears.'

'Well, I guess I am unclear as to why you are here before our committee,' states the Chair. 'Just who in the world are you?'

'Senator, have you ever been to a wedding?'

'Of course, many, many times. I attend one almost every weekend.'

'Then you will remember there comes that moment in the service when the bridegroom appears at the front of the congregation, just as everything is about to begin. Well, I am the one who has stood with the bridegroom and fixed his tie into a perfect shape. I am the friend who brushes the lint off of his tuxedo. I am the good friend who reminds him to smile at the bride as she comes down the aisle so she won't turn to him in 25 years and ask why he didn't smile on their wedding day. I am the one who whispers, "walk slowly", as he steps out, and I go to the back of the church to dim the lights so that only he can be seen. I am the one who shushes all the latecomers so they can hear his voice. I am simply the friend of the bridegroom, thanking God for the gift of serving him, and the privilege of getting out of the way.'

'Oh.'

Prayer

Help us to step back into the shadows, Bridegroom of all humanity, so that others might see you, hear your words, and rejoice that you have come to us at last. Amen

Third Monday of Advent

When my soul was embittered,
when I was pricked in heart,
I was stupid and ignorant;
I was like a brute beast toward you.
Nevertheless I am continually with you;
you hold my right hand.
You guide me with your counsel,
and afterward you will receive me with honour.
Whom have I in heaven but you?
And there is nothing on earth that I desire other than you.
My flesh and my heart may fail,
but God is the strength of my heart and my portion forever.

Indeed, those who are far from you will perish;
you put an end to those who are false to you.
But for me it is good to be near God;
I have made the Lord God my refuge,
to tell of all your works.

Psalm 73:21–28

Nearer than you think

As Dusty the Church Dog and I walked in the early-morning moonlight, we passed a young boy sitting on the bench at the corner, waiting in the dusky darkness for the school bus to pick him up. As we turned the corner and continued on down the street, about four houses down from the corner, we passed a woman standing at the end of her driveway. We said a good morning to each other, but her eyes never left the young man waiting at the corner. Just then, I heard the air brakes on the bus hiss as it stopped, and then it started on down the street. At that point, she smiled, whispering, 'okay', and went back into her house to continue her day.

When we lie in the hospital bed, groggy and recovering from the surgery, or lying awake in the middle of the night staring at the ceiling, wondering what word the doctor will bring when he makes his rounds, God is sitting in the corner, in that hard, uncomfortable chair (which could fold out into an even more painful bed if one chooses), keeping her eye on us, staying awake as long as we do, and even longer.

When we wander around the shelves in the always open store at the corner of Temptation and Wayward, finally going up to the counter to order one of those iced drinks filled to the brim with foolishness and wrong choices, Jesus paces back and forth outside on the sidewalk, pretending to look for change in the pay phone, acting for all the world as if he has nothing on his mind, just waiting to 'accidentally' bump into us as we walk out the door, knocking the drink out of our hands, letting it spill all over his front.

When the P.A. announces that the train is ready to board, we join the line, jostling and pushing, pulling our battered luggage on its rickety wheels, till we find our seat and wearily settle back for the ride, handing our ticket marked 'Anywhere But Here' to the conductor. And as we are just about to fall asleep, thinking no one has noticed or cares, Sophia comes along with her cart, asking, 'Something from the trolley, dearie?' as she hands us a sandwich and a little bottle of wine.

Wherever, whenever, however, God is always near.

Prayer

As near as that frosty breath as we walk outside; as close to us as the skin we wear; as constant as the beating of our heart in the quietest moments of the night – that is you, God in Community, and we thank you. Amen

Third Tuesday of Advent

The people who walked in darkness
have seen a great light;
those who lived in a land of deep darkness –
on them light has shined.
You have multiplied the nation,
you have increased its joy;
they rejoice before you
as with joy at the harvest,
as people exult when dividing plunder.
For the yoke of their burden,
and the bar across their shoulders,
the rod of their oppressor,
you have broken as on the day of Midian.
For all the boots of the tramping warriors
and all the garments rolled in blood
shall be burned as fuel for the fire.
For a child has been born for us,
a son given to us;
authority rests upon his shoulders;
and he is named
Wonderful Counselor, Mighty God,
Everlasting Father, Prince of Peace.
His authority shall grow continually,
and there shall be endless peace
for the throne of David and his kingdom.
He will establish and uphold it

with justice and with righteousness
from this time onward and forevermore.
The zeal of the Lord of hosts will do this …

But now thus says the Lord,
he who created you, O Jacob,
he who formed you, O Israel:
Do not fear, for I have redeemed you;
I have called you by name, you are mine.

Isaiah 9:2–7; 43:1

Before the comma

Jesus Christ, W.C.; M.G.; E.F.; PoP

According to Isaiah, this is the way that the business card or stationery for Jesus should read – with all his honorifics after the comma.

Or at least that is the way it would read if Jesus was as obsessed with what comes after the comma as we, and our culture, seem to be. There on the door, or on the nameplate on the desk, or in the brochure, or on the cover of the annual report are all those details about how well-educated we are, how honoured we are, how important we are (at least to ourselves).

Please don't misunderstand me. I know how hard folks work for such 'letters', for such an education, for such a title. It takes drive, determination, sacrifice, tenacity to reach those achievements. One of the reasons I did not go after a PhD is that I recognised that I did not have the qualities needed to pursue such a goal.

I have several certificates that have been framed for me – my degrees from college, as well as from the seminary I attended; the certificate attesting to my ordination as a Minister of Word and Sacrament. But I have this nagging feeling that what Jesus might be handing me to hang on my walls is a picture of Mother Teresa with her lined and weary face, which I am coming more and more to believe is what God looks like.

Now that I am at a different church, I am asked about how I want to be called – Reverend, Doctor, RevDoc, Mr? ... I have to admit that usually when someone calls me by those titles, I think they are talking to some-one else. While I prefer just plain Thom, I wouldn't mind being known as patient, compassionate, friend, chocolate-lover ...

And while I have 'earned' (whatever that means) the privilege of putting velvet bars on my robe, I am pretty sure that Jesus – the one who talked about giving away coats and cloaks, of clothing the naked, of being more concerned about the poor – might find that a little bit ostentatious, and probably looks askance at me at times.

For Jesus, it's far more important what we do before the comma. Do we reflect the love and care that went into the giving of our name? Do we carry on the heritage and hopes of those who stood before God and a faith community, naming us as God's own, God's beloved child?

Do we live out our relationship with Jesus, our Brother, our Friend, our Servant – who calls us to be sisters and brothers to the cast-offs of our society; who longs for us to befriend those whom the world hates; who sends us out from behind our desks, our homes, our titles to serve a creation that is broken and yearning for healing?

Prayer

Help us to realise that it is the life we live before the comma that makes all the difference for others, and for ourselves. In the name of the Prince of Peace, we pray. Amen

Third Wednesday of Advent

Praise the Lord!
How good it is to sing praises to our God;
for he is gracious, and a song of praise is fitting.
The Lord builds up Jerusalem;
he gathers the outcasts of Israel.
He heals the brokenhearted,
and binds up their wounds.
He determines the number of the stars;
he gives to all of them their names.
Great is our Lord, and abundant in power;
his understanding is beyond measure.
The Lord lifts up the downtrodden;
he casts the wicked to the ground.

Sing to the Lord with thanksgiving;
make melody to our God on the lyre.
He covers the heavens with clouds,
prepares rain for the earth,
makes grass grow on the hills.
He gives to the animals their food,
and to the young ravens when they cry.
His delight is not in the strength of the horse,
nor his pleasure in the speed of a runner;
but the Lord takes pleasure in those who fear him,
in those who hope in his steadfast love.

Psalm 147:1–11

Uncovering the path of praise

I don't know about you, but there are some days when I spend all my time muttering under my breath. Someone has e-mailed me an urban legend that I have seen a gazillion times. That publisher that just doesn't seem to understand the word 'no' calls again. A neighbour has taken MY parking space on the street. *muttermuttermutter* …

Of course, I am pretty good at grumbling. A committee has to revisit an issue that was already decided on months ago – even though everyone in the room knows nothing will change with another discussion. Politicians fill the airwaves with enough hot air to reduce my energy bill, if I could only plug my furnace into the TV. And my team did not make it into the big game! *grumblegrumblegrumble* …

And, sad to say, there are those moments when I am downright churlish. 'The light has changed, green means go – hello?!' I have been in the grocery line for 10 minutes, and the lane next to me opens, and the clerk takes those folks who have got into line after me! And, of course – the telemarketers who dial a dozen numbers at once: and you are standing there saying, 'Hello? Hell-O? HELLO?' while the caller decides if you are the lucky winner to listen to their spiel. *churlchurlchurl* …

But when I go to bed and reflect on the day, I always realise that I haven't done much praising, even when I had the chance. A 'V' of honking geese flew over me in the morning, and I was too busy muttering about how cold it was as I stooped down to get the newspaper. A neighbour waved 'hello' as she pulled out for work, and I was grumbling about the ice on the windshield. Two squirrels were chasing each other around and around the oak tree outside my office window, and I was ranting at the computer for taking its sweet time to power up.

If I am lucky, maybe when I sweep the snow off the sidewalk before I go to work this morning, I will uncover the path of praise.

> *praise God,*
> *all you birds*
>   *swooping down to*
>   *scoop up the seed*
>   *left out on the deck;*
> *praise him,*
>   *tail-twitching cat*
>   *stalking them from*
>   *behind the safety of*
>   *the dining room*
>   *window;*
> *praise the LORD!*
>
> *praise him,*
>   *you tireless dogs*
>   *chasing one another*
>   *round and round the yard*
>   *until a blizzard of loose*
>   *snow*
>   *swirls around you;*
>
> *praise God,*
>   *all you little kids*
>   *putting the carrot nose*

in the snow-teacher's face,
a book
in her hand;
praise the LORD!

praise God,
you fathers spending
Saturday morning baking
sugar cookies
with a gaggle of children,
not scolding
when more icing gets on
their faces than
on the bells and trees,
the sprinkles dotting
their cheeks
like freckles;

praise him,
all you mothers
who stay up until time
for Vigils,
assembling the race track
for your daughter,
putting the doll house
together for your
son;
praise the LORD!

Third Thursday of Advent

Ah, you who make iniquitous decrees,
who write oppressive statutes,
to turn aside the needy from justice
and to rob the poor of my people of their right,
that widows may be your spoil,
and that you may make the orphans your prey!
What will you do on the day of punishment,
in the calamity that will come from far away?
To whom will you flee for help,
and where will you leave your wealth,
so as not to crouch among the prisoners
or fall among the slain?
For all this his anger has not turned away;
his hand is stretched out still.

Isaiah 10:1–4

The most vulnerable in our midst

It was one of those comments that you take and stick in the back pocket of your mind. An executive director of a social service agency recently observed, in response to announced cutbacks in services through Medicaid and Medicare, 'The elderly are the new poor.'

Well, duh!

Older folks have always been one of our most vulnerable groups. And not just in our time and our culture, but more or less in every generation, in every community. That's why one of the Ten Commandments given at Sinai had to do with the elderly. According to biblical scholars, 'honour your father and mother' is not about being civil to your folks and eating your vegetables; it is about how a society takes care of its aging population.

The director's comment, though stating nothing new, is a reminder to all of us, but especially to those of us in faith communities (and those of us who believe we live in nations guided by belief in God), that in these uncertain and increasingly frightening economic times, it is the most vulnerable of our society who will be hit the hardest. Why? Because economic suffering always trickles down until it hits those folks who have no one below them to pass that suffering on to.

Those who are homeless, hungry and helpless are finding more people joining them in the lines at the food banks, at the soup kitchens, at the shelters. And those organisations are finding their sources of funding and donations decreasing exactly at the time when the need is so dramatically increasing.

Those who have no health insurance are finding health clinics closed, or one has to travel a greater distance to find an open clinic, which of course puts a greater strain on those who have no ready transportation choices. And if one has children, then the stress of trying to find some health care, any health care, for a sick child increases.

Vulnerable individuals like my son Teddy, who resides in a state developmental centre, may not even be aware that, or able to understand why, a lot of their friends are being moved out, and buildings are being closed, and staff (all those familiar faces who make them feel so safe) is being cut. In

Ohio, families recently received a letter informing them that the state has mandated that 725 individuals will need to be placed 'in community settings' (a phrase which basically means 'we don't know where they will end up'); this comes on top of previous 'decreases in population' which took place several months ago because of the economy. This means each of the ten centres will need to 'outsource' an average of 72 residents.

And all these changes in the lives of the most profoundly damaged, the most medically fragile individuals, will have a major impact on these children of God, especially those who do not have families or advocates to fight for them.

And anyone who is looking for assistance, be they already 'in the system' or those just discovering that such a system is in place, will find tighter, stricter regulations; fewer case managers; more hoops to jump through as the social service agencies deal with less and less funding, and more and more job cuts.

And, to no one's great surprise, there will be no $700 billion bailout for developmental centres, group homes, respite care for already-exhausted family caregivers. There will be no governmental loans to keep social workers and care managers on staff at the agencies that open their doors each morning to longer and longer lines. And the $1 trillion (!) being considered for rebuilding our 'infrastructure' will not be used for health clinics, for ERs, for food banks, for soup kitchens, for shelters for homeless families.

I know (because I hear them on radio and TV, and get mailings about their seminars) that there are those folks who are convinced that God was speaking about us and our current situation in books like Daniel and Revelation

– you know, all those 'hidden codes' about the End Times coming, the Apocalypse just over the horizon, the four horsemen throwing their saddles over their horses.

But for me, if God uses any writers in scripture to speak to us and our current situation, it is more folks like Isaiah, Amos and Hosea. Folks who tell about those times which will come when our compassion decreases as our fears increase; when our generosity falters as our income diminishes; when we turn away the poor and needy because whatever is in the cupboard is needed for us.

Prayer

As uncomfortable as it may make us, or as frustrated, you have always been clear that it is what we do for the most vulnerable in our midst that demonstrates our belief, our trust, our commitment to you, O God. So continue to speak those uncomfortable words, and hopes, to us through such folks as Isaiah, Amos and Hosea. Amen

Third Friday of Advent

I waited patiently for the Lord;
he inclined to me and heard my cry.
He drew me up from the desolate pit,
out of the miry bog,
and set my feet upon a rock,
making my steps secure.
He put a new song in my mouth,
a song of praise to our God.
Many will see and fear,
and put their trust in the Lord.
Happy are those who make
the Lord their trust,
who do not turn to the proud,
to those who go astray after false gods.
You have multiplied, O Lord my God,
your wondrous deeds and your thoughts toward us;
none can compare with you.

Psalm 40:1–5

Just ask Dusty

Everything I need to know about waiting I learned from Dusty the Church Dog.

There's *anticipation*, as he stands like a statue – not a twitch, not a sound, not a frozen breath into the air – as he waits, waits and waits for the squirrel to drop out of the tree, run over, and jump into his mouth.

There's *patience*, as he slowly lies down and stretches into a comfortable pose, settling into that long winter's nap, while I stop to chat with someone on our walk.

There's *expectation* as he comes down from his position on our bed, gets up on the couch and begins to stare out the window. When his ears begin to rise and his tail begins to twitch, I know it is just about time, and about 30 seconds later, Bonnie's car pulls into the driveway.

There's *excitement* as he runs back and forth from the table in front of the living room window to the front door, when he hears one of us answer the phone and say, 'Hi, Heather!', thinking she is just outside the door.

There is the *hope* evidenced as he raises first one eyebrow and then the other, almost as if he is sending some sort of Morse code to me, as the clock moves closer and closer to dinner time. And there is the pure, leaping-into-the-air, all-four-paws-off-the-ground-and-tail-brushing-the-ceiling *joy*, as I get up out of the chair and move towards the Dog Chow bucket.

There is that *trust*, as we sit in the exam room waiting for the vet to come in, Dusty curled underneath the bench, as close to my feet as he can get.

And there is the *sheer ecstasy* that comes with his head stuck out the back window, tongue and ears flying in the wind, as he strains to get his first glimpse of Teddy as we pull in front of the Broadview building.

There are all sorts of waiting … each and every one of them is perfect for Advent.

Just ask Dusty.

Prayer

Cats curled contentedly in the sunbeam; dogs listening, with one ear cocked, for the familiar footstep; crocuses nudging one another under winter's crust – all creation is teaching us about waiting, if we would only take the time to learn. Amen

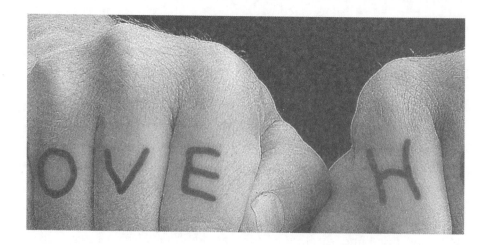

Third Saturday of Advent

For now we see in a mirror, dimly, but then we will see face to face. Now I know only in part; then I will know fully, even as I have been fully known.

1 Corinthians 13:12–13

I saw her face

We stood in the hallway of the church, me heading to my office to demystify myself, her putting on her coat, getting ready to head out into the bitter day. So, we had one of those hallway conversations folks often have as their minds are travelling in one direction, hoping this brief stop won't slow them down too much.

I asked how her Christmas had been and she asked about mine. We had gone up to Columbus to see Teddy, to go out for our now traditional Christmas repast at the Waffle House, indulging in the major food group known as sugar. She had spent the holy day with her cat, but was off to a relative's house this afternoon where she would be immersed in a pool of 40 or so relatives.

We both bemoaned the commercialism of Christmas, the overindulgence of children and grandchildren who end up with a ton of presents, the toys that get broken so quickly and easily and end up out on the curb the week after the holiday. And we both recalled how, as kids, sometimes the biggest excitement in the neighbourhood came when someone had a major appliance delivered to their house, and the empty cardboard box was set out by the curb, and was immediately turned into an aeroplane, pirate ship, mansion, truck, whatever and wherever our imagination would take us.

That's when she mentioned the fact that when she was growing up, in a family with 12 kids, there were no individual gifts given at Christmas, but there was a group gift for all the kids – a board game, a puzzle, a book, something to be shared by all. And then, with the memory glittering in her eyes, she told me about the Christmas when her six sisters were all adults, and she gave each of them her very own colouring book and a box of crayons. A gift that they could never have had as a child, a memory they shared from their childhood, a surprise they never expected now that they were all grown up. 'Oh, I wish you could have seen the looks on their faces when they opened those presents!' she said.

No need: I saw her face.

Prayer

In the candlelit faces of children in the church pageant, in the glistening tears on the cheeks of the great-grandmother holding the newest member of the family, in the laugh-lined eyes of the neighbour dropping off a tin of homemade cookies, we see you, Advent's Wonder, even as you come looking for us. Amen

Fourth week of Advent

Fourth Sunday of Advent

A shoot shall come out from the stump of Jesse,
and a branch shall grow out of his roots.
The spirit of the Lord shall rest on him,
the spirit of wisdom and understanding,
the spirit of counsel and might,
the spirit of knowledge and the fear of the Lord.
His delight shall be in the fear of the Lord.

He shall not judge by what his eyes see,
or decide by what his ears hear;
but with righteousness he shall judge the poor,
and decide with equity for the meek of the earth;
he shall strike the earth with the rod of his mouth,
and with the breath of his lips he shall kill the wicked.
Righteousness shall be the belt around his waist,
and faithfulness the belt around his loins.

The wolf shall live with the lamb,
the leopard shall lie down with the kid,
the calf and the lion and the fatling together,
and a little child shall lead them.
The cow and the bear shall graze,
their young shall lie down together;
and the lion shall eat straw like the ox.
The nursing child shall play over the hole of the asp,
and the weaned child shall put its hand on the adder's den.

They will not hurt or destroy
on all my holy mountain;
for the earth will be full of the knowledge of the Lord
as the waters cover the sea.

Isaiah 11:1–9

Do we remember?

Years ago, I was visiting friends who were getting ready to move into a new home. We were over at the new house one day, painting and such, when the former owner stopped by to pick up some things. At one point, I looked out the window, and there was the fellow, his hand resting on an old tree, just standing there. My friend Robert, who noticed what I was looking at, simply said, 'He's remembering, and thanking the tree.'

At the time, I thought to myself, *What?*

But as I look at the empty space that stands where our tree used to tower into the sky, as my eyes are drawn to the fresh stump (that even seems to glow in the dark), I finally understand. The sweetgum tree, which was damaged in the hurricane back in September, finally had to be cut down; it was just too broken, too shaky, too much of a danger.

But I remember: I remember the tree that stood and watched over Teddy and his friends, and the church's youth group, as they bounced higher and higher into the sky on the trampoline. I remember the old tyre-swing that hung on the sturdy branch long after Teddy had outgrown it, yet the tree was always ready to give a little kid a ride. I remember the cool shade of its leafy branches on hot days after mowing the lawn. I remember the comforting sound of the Spirit moving through the branches on crisp fall evenings.

As I stare into the empty space, and try to avoid the stumpy reminder of our loss, I remember, and I give thanks.

Isaiah says that from the stumps of our toppled efforts, God will bring a time when the meek and the poor will finally find the justice we seem unable to offer.

Isaiah says that from our failed attempts at peace and reconciliation, God will bring forth a kingdom where the worst enemies share bunk beds at night, and where the person who has hurt us the most will hand us the bread of Life and the cup of Grace.

Isaiah tells us that as we stare into the empty spaces where our comfort and strength once towered, God will come and fill us with that joy which has no end, with that hope which holds us up when we are about to fall over, with that Spirit who is our constant companion and caregiver when everyone else has wandered off.

Isaiah tells us …

… but do we remember?

Prayer

God of trees and stumps, help us to remember, and in that remembering, to give thanks. And in that thanksgiving, to look for the newness you are bringing into our lives. Amen

Fourth Monday of Advent

Now the birth of Jesus the Messiah took place in this way. When his mother Mary had been engaged to Joseph, but before they lived together, she was found to be with child from the Holy Spirit. Her husband Joseph, being a righteous man and unwilling to expose her to public disgrace, planned to dismiss her quietly. But just when he had resolved to do this, an angel of the Lord appeared to him in a dream and said, 'Joseph, son of David, do not be afraid to take Mary as your wife, for the child conceived in her is from the Holy Spirit. She will bear a son, and you are to name him Jesus, for he will save his people from their sins.' All this took place to fulfil what had been spoken by the Lord through the prophet: 'Look, the virgin shall conceive and bear a son, and they shall name him Emmanuel,' which means, "God is with us."

Matthew 1:18–23

You come

you come,
    struggling through
    the deep drifts of our sins,
       to pull us out,
       hand us a warm toddy of grace,
         and wrap us in
         the comfort of
           your hope;

you come,
    unlatching the storm windows

84

we have hung over our
hopelessness,
    so we can open our hearts
    to the bracing breath
    of your joy;

you come,
    you arms full of groceries,
    cooking up a storm,
        letting us lick the bowls,
        and decorate the kitchen
        with icing and sprinkles,
    then sending us out
    with our arms full
    of your goodness,
        so everyone might
        gorge themselves
            on your love;

you come,
    that little child
    taking our hand
    on a cold winter night's
        walk,
    suddenly stopping
    and whispering,
        'did you hear that?'

o come, o come,
    Emmanuel.

Fourth Tuesday of Advent

When Joseph awoke from sleep, he did as the angel of the Lord commanded him; he took her as his wife, but had no marital relations with her until she had borne a son; and he named him Jesus.

Matthew 1:24–25

Standing in the background

We usually find him stuck back in the corner of the crèche set. He may be kneeling, he may be standing, he may appear as if he has a rather stunned look on his face. And in the Christmas pageant at most churches, he never has any lines to say, never gets a solo, never has the spotlight turned on him.

Poor Joseph.

And how much poorer we are, because we believe that Joseph has no role to play, no big part, nothing to say or sing during these holiest of days. Oh, we convince ourselves that we don't need to pay any attention to him, or shouldn't, because (we whisper behind our hands, just as his neighbours probably did) he's not really the father of the child. He is just a bystander, a person to ignore, a character actor who appears just for a moment, and then is forgotten.

But is there any better person to model trust for us?

Sure, he could have easily dismissed what had been told him one night as a dyspeptic dream caused by all the rich food at the office party. Yet, Joseph saw it as his calling, and decided that he would do whatever it was God was asking him to do.

And couldn't we use a little more trust in our lives, in our communities, in our world, in our churches right now?

And courage?

Imagine: to stand up to family, friends, drinking buddies, and probably even strangers who had heard only the gossip, and simply say, perhaps over and over, 'Whatever. I stand by Mary. I believe her, I love her, I will marry her, I will help her to raise this child.' Couldn't we use the reminder that courage is a trait we need as we move into those unknown moments – a new job, a new year, children, retirement, downsizing?

What about his lifelong commitment to Mary, to Jesus, to the rest of the kids who came along?

He could have become an absentee father, he could have been one of those dads constantly being searched for to pay child support. But he goes about his job, working long hours, providing for Mary and the family, helping to put food on the table and a roof over their heads. He reminds us of our calling to get up out of bed each morning, and simply go about doing all that day-to-day stuff we do as fathers and mothers, as teachers and volunteers, as friends and neighbours – all those little, insignificant tasks we take on, while standing in the background, no one noticing us, but making all the difference in the world to someone.

This year, let's reach back into that shadowy corner of the crèche where we have stuck him, and move Joseph up to the manger where he belongs.

Prayer

With angels singing, the shepherds rejoicing, the wise ones gifting, it is easy to overlook Joseph, Everlasting Father. But since he is the one who most resembles us, we give you thanks for his trust, his courage, his loyalty, his role in this holy story. Amen

Fourth Wednesday of Advent

The Lord said:
Because these people draw near with their mouths
and honour me with their lips,
while their hearts are far from me,
and their worship of me is a human commandment
learned by rote;
so I will again do
amazing things with this people,
shocking and amazing.

Isaiah 29:13–14

And in the spirit he carried me away to a great, high mountain and showed me the holy city Jerusalem coming down out of heaven from God. It has the glory of God and a radiance like a very rare jewel, like jasper, clear as crystal. It has a great, high wall with twelve gates, and at the gates twelve angels, and on the gates are inscribed the names of the twelve tribes of the Israelites; on the east three gates, on the north three gates, on the south three gates, and on the west three gates. And the wall of the city has twelve foundations, and on them are the twelve names of the twelve apostles of the Lamb …

I saw no temple in the city, for its temple is the Lord God the Almighty and the Lamb. And the city has no need of sun or moon to shine on it, for the glory of God is its light, and its lamp is the Lamb. The nations will walk by its light, and the kings of the earth will bring their glory into it. Its gates will never be shut by day – and there will be no night there.

Revelation 21:10–14, 22–25

The open gates

An old sci-fi story tells about a crew that has landed on Mars. They are surprised to find that the air is breathable. They are shocked when a scout comes back to report that a town has been found. As the crew rushes to explore, they are even more amazed that the streets, the houses are just like those back on Earth. One by one, each astronaut finds a house that is populated by family from back home. Is it a mass delusion perpetrated by the Martians, or is it heaven, since the family members are all those who have died?

For centuries humans, and especially believers, have struggled with the idea of life after death, of heaven. What would it look like, feel like, be like? For some, because of the descriptions in today's passage from Revelation, it is a wonderful, bejeweled city, with streets paved in gold, with beauty that can only be hinted at by John.

For others, heaven will be that place where all pain is healed, all tears are wiped away, all the broken people will be made whole, where someone like my son Teddy will become the person God intended before others and the world damaged him.

While I still remember the vivid dream I had as a teenager of heaven being that place where I am invited to step out of the crowd and lead the marching band from the movie *The Music Man*, I am now hoping that I will instead find a great big library (with no due dates), a comfortable rocking chair, lots of pastries, and an unlimited supply of chocolates. I would guess each of us has that place, that person, that hope, that joy we hope we will find when Jesus returns to take us home on the occasion of the Second Advent.

But amid all conversations about heaven being the place where only 'certain' folks will go; amid all the dogma about some being destined (pre- or not) for that other place (where one certainly will not find much to enjoy); in the midst of a culture that seems to be so wrapped up in who will be left behind that we cannot see those who are being left behind right now, I notice one verse in particular in this passage:

'Its gates will never be shut by day – and there will be no night there.'

If the gates of the New Jerusalem are never shut, then it seems to me that we are being reminded, at the very end of scripture, that God is going to make it possible for everyone to come home. And if there is no night, but only day, then aren't we being told that even those who have lived in the deepest shadows can find their way to God's heart and hopes for them?

We have become so convinced that we know what heaven will be like and just exactly who God will let in there, but we may be just like those folks at the first Advent, who were so surprised, shocked and amazed when God showed up in a barn, surrounded by dirt and grime, being born as a little baby into a working-class family who would soon be hunted by the authorities.

Maybe, just maybe, when it comes to heaven, life beyond death, and the second Advent, God will do exactly what he says through Isaiah – something so shocking and amazing we might not even recognise it.

Prayer

In the quiet of this day and night, as we wait to celebrate in an almost mundane way the shocking way in which you came to Bethlehem so long ago, keep our hearts, our minds, our hopes open to the amazement which you still have in store for us, Approaching God. Amen

Fourth Thursday of Advent

For you shall go out in joy,
and be led back in peace;
the mountains and the hills before you
shall burst into song,
and all the trees of the field shall clap their hands.
Instead of the thorn shall come up the cypress;
instead of the brier shall come up the myrtle;
and it shall be to the Lord for a memorial,
for an everlasting sign that shall not be cut off.

Isaiah 55:12–13

No pity-parties, please

Don't you just hate some of the stunts God pulls?

I was all set to have a big Pity Party. After all, it had been 20 years since I was ordained as a Minister of the Word and Sacrament. It was one of those 'mountaintop' moments: family and friends, a special anthem by the choir, sermon by my ministry-mentor, a big luncheon, lots of feel-good moments.

And on the 20th anniversary? Well, I got up and put the laundry in the machine; cleaned up the hairball the cat had left on the floor; had my usual bowl of Cheerios and fruit; found more grey hair in my head and beard; came to the office, where the stacks of unsolved issues and things undone were still waiting for me.

No cards, no calls, no party, no pats on the back, no Sgt Pepper or any other band marching around in the parking lot of the church. No one telling me how wonderful I am, or how much I have done for them. No e-mail from *Time Magazine* requesting to interview me as one of the top preachers in the country. No call from *The Today Show* to comment on the latest crisis. It seemed that no one noticed, or cared. Boohoo hoo! Poor me, poor me, poor me.

Then, I sat down to write my poem/prayer for the back of the Sunday's bulletin, and the Holy Spirit reminded me of what this day and every day, what ministry, is all about:

> i would prefer
>   to be
>   leaning against the wall,
> shuffling my two left feet,
>   watching the world
>   twirl by;
> but you take me by the hand
>   to teach me
>   the dance steps
>   of grace;
>
> when i walk near
>   the piano,
>   it shudders,
>   hoping
>   i will not sit down;
> but you take my fingers

and place them on the keys,
    whispering,
    'play, play with joy, play!'

even with
    the biggest bucket,
    i can't carry a tune;
  but you push me
      out onto the stage,
    introducing me as
  the new soloist
    in the Good News Choir.

i will celebrate your joy,
  sing your hope,
    play your love,
    leaping and whirling
  in your grace
    for ever!

Fourth Friday of Advent

Sing for joy, O heavens, and exult, O earth;
break forth, O mountains, into singing!
For the Lord has comforted his people,
and will have compassion on his suffering ones.
But Zion said, 'The Lord has forsaken me,
my Lord has forgotten me.'
Can a woman forget her nursing-child,
or show no compassion for the child of her womb?
Even these may forget,
yet I will not forget you.
See, I have inscribed you on the palms of my hands;
your walls are continually before me.

Isaiah 49:13–16

God's hands

In the 1955 film *The Night of the Hunter*, Robert Mitchum plays Harry Powell, a self-professed preacher who has the word HATE tattooed on the backs of the fingers of his left hand, while the word LOVE is imprinted on the backs of the fingers of his right hand. He uses his hands to tell the story of the conflict between good and evil, and how good always triumphs in this eternal struggle. A spellbinding speaker, he convinces folks that he is a 'man of God', but the movie watcher knows that Powell is in reality a sadistic serial killer, come to town to find a large sum of money hidden by an ex-cellmate who was hanged for his crime.

There are some who are convinced that this is what God's hands are like – that when God reaches out, it is with a clenched fist, the fingers of one hand marked WRATH which will be used to punish all those who don't look like us, talk like us, believe like us, act like us ... It is the fist which will grasp all those who don't live according to 'God's way' and will be cast into the shadows of eternity. Oh, don't worry, there is that other hand of God's, with the fingers marked LOVE. But it is extended to just a select few (and we all know who they are, don't we?).

God's hands are the hands of a baby, constantly reaching out to everything and everyone, wanting to grasp them, and learn more about the wonders of the world. God's hands are the hands of a worker, calloused and paint-stained from building the kingdom of peace and reconciliation. God's hands are the hands of a nurse, who wipes the feverish brow and cradles the newborn. God's hands are engraved with our faces on the palms, so that when God washes up, we are constantly held before those compassionate eyes.

And when God reaches out to take us by the heart to draw us still closer, we see that on the backs of God's fingers are the words LOVE and HOPE, and we know that we will be held for ever.

Prayer

You lie in the manger, waving your hands around, wanting to take hold of us; you reach out your hands to take us with you on this journey to the kingdom; you open your hands to be scarred so our lives might be healed. May we open our hands to cradle your love and hope, until we have the opportunity to hand them on to another. Amen

Christmas Eve

While they were there, the time came for her to deliver her child. And she gave birth to her firstborn son and wrapped him in bands of cloth, and laid him in a manger, because there was no place for them in the inn.

Luke 2:6–7

You came

you could have
come
as warrior, ready
to take us on
one at a time
or en masse …

you could have
come
a whirlwind
swirling, twirling,
twisting around us,
flinging us up into
the air …

you could have
come
with a bag of
chocolates

in one hand
and
a time-out chair
in the other;

you came
a tiny
vulnerable
baby
lungs screaming for
life,
fingers grasping for
something to hold on to,
your whole being
completely depending on
us (!) to
feed you
change you
clothe you
protect you
love you

and we were

gobsmacked.

Christmas Day

For the grace of God has appeared, bringing salvation to all, training us to renounce impiety and worldly passions, and in the present age to live lives that are self-controlled, upright, and godly, while we wait for the blessed hope and the manifestation of the glory of our great God and Saviour, Jesus Christ. He it is who gave himself for us that he might redeem us from all iniquity and purify for himself a people of his own who are zealous for good deeds.

Titus 2:11–14

Morning grace

the angels have folded
their sheet music
and stored it away
for another year,
   twittering away
   about the ski trip
   planned for New Year's;

the shepherds are all
snug in their beds,
thoughts of last night
distracting them from
much-needed sleep,

while the kids play
quietly in the next room
(with an occasional, very loud
'SHUSH! You'll wake them!');

Mary turns to Joseph
in the midst of packing
for the trip,
 grumbling,
 'Wise ones, huh?
not smart enough
to bring something practical
 like a crib or nappies?'

Jesus lies quietly
in the manger,
smiling up at the cow
whose great big eyes
brim with care,
 as he rests up
 for the work of Christmas:

weaning us from sin;
holding our hand as
 we take those first
 teetering steps in the kingdom;

clapping his hands in delight
when we first whisper
    'abba';
helping us to wrap up
grace, peace and joy,
    re-gifting them
    for the folks down
    at the hopeless shelter.

Notes

'Love, Hope' photo © David Coleman. David Coleman is a minister of the United Reformed Church in Greenock, jobsharing with Zam Walker. He is a photographer, a digital artist, and a member of the Iona Community.

Wild Goose Publications is part of the Iona Community, which is:

- An ecumenical movement of men and women from different walks of life and different traditions in the Christian church
- Committed to the gospel of Jesus Christ, and to following where that leads, even into the unknown
- Engaged together, and with people of goodwill across the world, in acting, reflecting and praying for justice, peace and the integrity of creation
- Convinced that the inclusive community we seek must be embodied in the community we practise

Together with our staff, we are responsible for:

- Our islands residential centres of Iona Abbey, the MacLeod Centre on Iona, and Camas Adventure Centre on the Ross of Mull

and in Glasgow:

- The administration of the Community
- Our work with young people
- Our publishing house, Wild Goose Publications
- Our association in the revitalising of worship with the Wild Goose Resource Group

The Iona Community was founded in Glasgow in 1938 by George MacLeod, minister, visionary and prophetic witness for peace, in the context of the poverty and despair of the Depression. Its original task of rebuilding the monastic ruins of Iona Abbey became a sign of hopeful rebuilding of community in Scotland and beyond. Today, we are about 250 Members, mostly in Britain, and 1500 Associate Members, with 1400 Friends worldwide. Together and apart, 'we follow the light we have, and pray for more light'.

For information on the Iona Community contact:
The Iona Community, Fourth Floor, Savoy House, 140 Sauchiehall Street,
Glasgow G2 3DH, UK. Phone: 0141 332 6343
admin@iona.org.uk   www.iona.org.uk

For enquiries about visiting Iona, please contact:
Iona Abbey, Isle of Iona, Argyll PA76 6SN, UK. Phone: 01681 700404
ionacomm@iona.org.uk